TRASH CAN MAN

by

Christopher Alexander Berg

CCB Publishing
British Columbia, Canada

Trash Can Man

Copyright ©2020 by Christopher Alexander Berg
ISBN-13   978-1-77143-413-3
First Edition

Library and Archives Canada Cataloguing in Publication
Title: Trash can man / by Christopher Alexander Berg.
Names: Berg, Christopher Alexander, 1978- author.
Description: Poems.
Identifiers: Canadiana 20200200569 | ISBN 9781771434133 (softcover)
Classification: LCC PS3602.E72 T73 2020 | DDC 811/.6—dc23

Cover artwork design by: Christopher Alexander Berg

Publisher: CCB Publishing
              British Columbia, Canada
              www.ccbpublishing.com

ACT I

REFLECTION

Is being human an excuse for being cruelest

of all creatures?

Fluid in all features

involving a kill.

"Rooting for grim reapers."

I don't blame you
for not wanting
the world to know
you know me.

Please show me

a way home

and I'll go bleed

there.

Need air...

"It's stuffy."

Stuffing ...,

bodies in a box.

"Merry Christmas."

We're not in this (together)

Soon to witness ...

the end.

Plan's going accordingly ...

No sorting me (out)

Divorcing the

human side of me.

Crying myself to sleep

(for the last time)

Gonna cast my (sins away)

Felt enough hate

(for multiple lifetimes)

Dysfunctional retries

continuous ...

"Combustible bloodlines."

What if I'm the divine feminine?

Tried for innocence ...

and found guilty.

To die, my sentence.

"Oh well."

"Guess I'll get to leave early,

... and miss the apocalypse."

Twist of a novelist, (gone rogue)

All's now opposite

(of what's expected)

Cut's infected.

"Burn it."

Digressing (here)

"Back to beheadings."

Back to red weddings.

Seed setting...,

(by force)

All getting ... (reality)

No balancing (this act)

This back...,

(full of daggers)

Does it matter at all?

Baby batter

marking ...,

one face after another.

After the buzzer,

the shot dropped.

"Won't count."

Actors with rubber (souls) unite.

"Got a world to stain."

Can any of us outlast

the past troubles that affect us?

Is there a magic necklace (somewhere?)

"A magic headdress?"

Only a miracle we have left to
believe in.

Double teamed in

screams ... running ...,

trying to flee
demons.

"I think we're all cast outs now."

Dragged out...,

of bounds.

(No flags out)

Must pass now ... away.

"I'm gassed out."

Human? Are we?

There's monsters here.

(Imposters)

"Hell is empty."

Roster's (full) of ringers.

"We don't stand a chance."

Bringers ... of death and grief.

(The demons are here)

Legions ...

of many. (Cretins...,

walking ... in droves)

Whispering now

(to myself)

"Am I

being too loud?"

Look at me now...

"Who is this?"

New witness, please?

"It's not Chris."

I'm not this ...

individual.

A residual (is needed)

... / ritual.

Past principles ...

(gone now)

Stacked intervals ...,

control.

Looking both ways ...

on a one way.

Checking all lanes.

"I don't trust anyone."

Any fun (we have here)

will add tears

later on.

Made a bomb (last night)

"Sang a song,

of peace."

Have to look down to see myself.

Have to get out from beneath.

Jump off the end.

"Come on!"

Hunts on again.

No longer in

your grip.

Got bombs to send

to everyone.

"Priorities."

Cries whoring me (out)

"Transforming me."

Restoring me (back)

to my true self.

Gonna sue Hell

for being here...

Too many demons here.

"What's happened to humanity?"

Screw sanity ...,

don't need it.

Can't be the (hero anymore)

Can't keep these
feelings to myself.

Killing just for health (reasons)

Only time will tell ...

who the villains are.

"History changes."

(Vanishes)

Plenty deranged

individuals

in high places.

Seems we've all painted (ourselves)

into a corner.

Placing orders ...

for tortur-
ing devices.

Facing shorter ...

lifespans everywhere.

About to lose it ...,

my mind.

"May have already."

No day here steady.

Most people ... messy ... (pieces of shit)

Betting on scripts

to change hearts.

Resting in grips ..., of killers.

(Soon to get crushed)

Doomed because of

our original sin.

A convincible win

for the bad guys...

War criminals in (my cum)

"Now you know how the darkness feels."

(All targets here)

Most heartless.

No more roles to play in the future.

(No future)

No more holes to bang.

Prove your human

and bleed.

I'm seen,

only in nightmares.

Right where (I belong)

Time tears (holes) in all.

Knives care

for no one.

A dried up ocean, I am.

Cried too much

for a world

that gives no fucks.

I feel like hiding from everyone.

Best we come

to some sort of conclusion.

No use in

getting mad anymore.

All screwed in (this game)

No train of thought helpful

(when going insane)

Feel like Ichabod Crane ...

running from the horseman.

Except I'm the horseman

running ... from Ichabod Crane.

Another long day (in this battle)

Another wrong way.

Got somewhere to be?

"No."

"Just somewhere to leave."

Disconnecting
from a world
that needs
to be
disconnected from.

Can't believe
where we're at now...

Going back now, (to silence)

"My army of aborted would take over the world."

"We have the numbers."

All races under

one flag

and god.

One mad (king)
after the next.

After conquest,

death ...,

will greet those
that left (us)
in garbage bags.

Arms are scabbed (up)

Parts are bad...

(Need a makeover)

"Got a takeover to plan."

Not in me

to care right now.

Got plenty ..., reasons why.

Reasons I

know will never bring me

peace inside.

Be that I

am thankful here.

Homicide

awaits me.

Demons chase me ...,

non stop.

Jesus, take the (gun)

cause I'm not

myself today.

A crowd awaits

and not a single face

I care for.

About to instigate

a nightmare.

Might bare

my soul today.

Might tear it in half.

Can't save 'em (all)

Can't change 'em.

In flames we'll

realize our mistakes.

Calling for a state (of emergency)

Need a grand escape.

"Will the clocks ever tick

in our favor?"

No waivers here (or) life savers.

Just traitors (with)

straight razors.

Behavior (justified)

Brush aside ... loose ground.

Customized (destruction)

"Times winding down for lots of things."

Gun shots fill dreams

and reality.

Beastiality ...,

next to go mainstream.

Think we

may have jumped the shark.

Lumped the dark (together)

Flunked the art ...

of war.

We've got a grave to get in ...

(American made)

No chairs at this ta-
ble.

Just terrorist labels.

Unable (to be human)

Think I'm gonna flee...

Got things

to look out for.

(Got needs)

Lost dreams

in a nightmare.

Lost me

(as well)

This event is
wrapping up.

Start packing up
the equipment.

Must get the
fuck out of here.

Non existence ...,

coming.

The dumbing (down)

of all is

nearly complete.

Fear it may be

too late

for there to be peace.

Where will we sleep

if the ground falls?

"Hope we'll have wings."

Am I tearing in half

or coming together?

Hunting for treasure

(in a mind field)

Fucking the better

side of me.

Can't hide a thing

(from myself)

No privacy.

A lie to think

I would ever be something

that tries to be

itself.

Is mercy possible?

Obstacles ... everywhere.

(Nothing optional)

Call an audible, please!

Extinction,

probable.

We are the last of the least.

Marks of beasts (on us)

Part deceased

we all are

but all stars

in charts released

that condemn us.

Please bend the

rules (slightly)

Unkindly (acts)

grow wildly.

Looking for somewhere
to belong at.

These rules stacked

against me.

(Hear ghouls laugh)

Just cruel facts

in the making.

I'm shaking,

trying to be still.

Trying to fulfill

(hallucinations)

Seeing demons

(everywhere)

breeding.

More bleeding to come.

More screaming.

More beatings.

More treasonous bums.

More fleeing

(war zones)

Outlived by insects ...

We're all next (for something)

Must all beg

forgiveness.

Incentives

for evil (committed)

Not in this

(together)

"Defenseless."

Defeated ...

All heated (arguments)

these days.

All deep in (shit)

Leaned on quick (sand)

disguised as brick.

Surprised I didn't

see this coming.

"We die to live."

We cry in hid-
den spots.

We once were kids.

Just feels like
this isn't me.

Almost being someone
or something ... (else)

What the hell
is going on here?

Something's odd here.

Twilight Zone's lost here, too.

Holocaust near ... x 8.

All taped (together)

with eyes shut.

(All raped together)

The sane just ... offed themselves.

Tossed themselves

right off the edge ... of sanity.

Vanity ...,

(our downfall)

Planning things

for town hall ... (meetings)

"Time to kill demons."

Eating ... this world alive.

Needed for balance.

Challenged ...,

always.

Valiant efforts made...

(with no success)

Our bones are next

(to fossilize)

Sodomized

at a young age.

"Modernized."

Saw your eyes (peeking)

"Colonized."

Who decides the outcomes?

Outdone again...

(Outrun)

I see the end of the dream coming.

(The end of a means to a way)

I'd scream but afraid

the cretins will hear me.

I'd leave but the same (kind)

of people are everywhere.

February stars

look warm up there.

Deformed and bare (to the world)

I'll try to care

tomorrow...

if I get through today.

Speechless ... (with the most to say)

"I guess it's time to worry now."

A hurry now, we're all in

(wearing out welcomes)

I tried perfection

but can't do it.

(Have no reflection)

Failed inspection (at birth)

"Didn't have the last name."

Insert vision here ...

(Insert wisdom)

In dirt. Victims,

we all are.

Alert! System

overload ...

Parts unknown

we're at ...,

calling it home.

Saying we own (the night)

to an army of clones.

Blowing our loads (together)

on a pile of bones.

Scars on saviors...

Does the caged bird

sing or cry?

Looking forward to A.I.

taking over.

Had enough of this.

All these ruffians (about)

All this suffering.

The procedure's over.

Got needs for clovers

(with 4 leafs)

A roller coaster,

we're jumping from.

Polar opposites

of everything.

(Solar hostages)

This is not a test.

It's reality ...

on balconies

of castles.

Born battling (demons)

"More cavalry needed."

Trash Can Man

Not keeping

any promises.

(Just secrets)

Not seeing

a bright side here.

All grieving

for sanity (and the loss of it)

Got nothing (to talk about)

Bots coming ...

We need a cleansing.

We're all pretending (anyway)

No more defending

(these crimes)

Cream pies (inside us)

Knee high ...,

to dirt.

Throwing Nerf (balls)

to crowds

(with bombs in them)

So long to them (all)

"Telethon for 'em."

Here's a song for 'em

(called)

"Goodbye."

I spy

writing on the wall.

Fighting for a cause

(that's lost)

Never an applause.

"Maybe I need a makeover."

These game overs (are getting to me)

No sane shoulder

to cry on.

All eyes on (prizes)

we won't have.

Lost sight on (meaning)

"I'm fine with being the villain."

(Got time for scheming)

Thinking we have forever.

"We don't."

The better years behind us...

(Just beggar's tears left)

We never said "yes" to this.

We never got set (before go)

We all know

the outcome...

but just won't

admit it.

"Death sentence written."

We're finished.

One more mile to go.

One more vacation (till the world ends)

One more kiss.

One more defensive (strategy)

One more twist

(to this conclusion)

Contusions (on our souls)

"Amusement for demons."

Heard voices (again)

"Never joyous."

Too much poison (in the air)

Too much hoisting

(of false gods)

A soft spot (I have)

for mental cases.

Close to wasting

many ...

Close to breaking

down ...

A triple threat now ...

French kissing,

as clips empty.

(Script's ending)

Conspire (against me)

you all do

and all use (disguises)

(disguised as)

half truths.

I'm not who

I used to be.

I'm worse than he

(ever was)

Hat and glove (ready)

The next Freddy (Krueger)

The next levee ...

(to break)

Saw a snake
with my face (on it)

Saw a gaping hole
in its head.

Wrote a last will and testa-
ment at 15.

No prom queens my way ...
or prom kings.

Do all things
come with a catch?

Tattooing things

that reach out.

Gluing wings

to my back.

"One way or another."

Through a drop

or a cover (of darkness)

Gonna part this

venue now.

"Continues out ...,

and on my last man."

Saw a trash can

(with my name on it)

representing,

a last stand.

No facts can

tell the truth ...

or bare a burden.

Just know we're hurting...

(everywhere)

"Just hope it's worth it."

Please just turn the

TV off ...

"Heard enough of the chatter."

Do all lives really matter?

"It doesn't seem that way."

Bumming dreams (from)

what others say.

My mother chained (me up)

so other things

(could take over)

Made owner (of)

a lonely heart.

"An empty cart

(sitting)

a world apart."

Here now ...

There now ...

Gone.

Not strong enough for this.

Not long before I snap.

Sliding back ...

(to my old self)

No soul's helped

(by hatred)

No cold melts (away)

What made us this way?

How can we be
so hateful?

I'm unable to

process it.

The cost of this (is)

everything.

Every came (and went)

now gone with ...

every name we lived.

Can't help the helpless...,

cause we're the helpless.

No god can tell us (anything)

We killed him

and built new beings (to worship)

A new queen (mother)

We're not brothers anymore...

We're mother fuckers.

"In a test tube."

Filling rubbers,

with blood.

All of

the immeasurable now.

Just skeletal (creatures)

made edible...

Not credible (enough)

for anything ...

Intellectually (flawed)

Crisscrossed ...

No send offs

(for my kind)

Just sent off.

Have lift off

in 10, 9 ...

Stand by ...,

there's commotion.

Heard explosions!

Bad omens and Trojan horses
surround us ...

We're nouns just

connected to verbs.

Hoping our words

reach something

before the earth turns

to blood.

Shunned ...

by most.

Done (before starting)

Someone push the reset (button)

"I think it's time for recess."

See less (than we used to)

"Seem less."

"Too many rodents in the world."

"Too many hijacked
      individuals."

Gone are original

(motherfuckers)

Condition?

"Critical."

Non livable,

this surface ...

Just may be
the worst this
planet has seen.

Standing are we?

Together?

Dancing with severed legs.

Better head

(for the exits)

Never said
they were open.

"The brighter the picture
the darker the negative."

Direction we're headed in,

worries me ...

Blurry we are
to rainbows
and promises.

Thirsty we are ...,

for death.

Steered for user (friendly devices)

"Cleared for shooters."

No newer (versions)

available ...

Much fewer (soon)

The beginning of the end began long ago.

Here we are now in the middle of our destruction.

No suction cups here
to rid things ...

Always something going on.

Always running from the bombs

(but about to run to them)

Gotta prove 'em all wrong ... or right.

All gone with time ...

"No more service here."

(We're closed)

"The end's coming...,

and it needs a soundtrack."

Not reaching

for any hand

other than my own.

(Trying to phone home)

Where will my bones (rest?)

"Where should they?"

Just cold shoulders

(to lean on)

High beams on ...,

looking for a victim.

"No vacancy."

I'm taking the
high road here.

"Don't wait for me."

Not savoring
the moments, I guess.

Just pray for me.

Must break from the

rules outside.

(Escape with me)

Door's not open

to anyone ...

Not quoting

(bible verses here)

Just spiral-ing

out of control.

"Seeing the whole (world) on fire."

(Thinking it's cold)

Needing a pole

(to vault on)

"Too many swords here

to fall on."

All guns

pointed at me.

(Both hands full)

"Thought they said we we're
equal here."

All people here

aren't we?

Start the (countdown now)

Less heartbeats pound

within chests.

Within necks

blades lie.

All sins checked (off)

Played hide (and seek)

with a changed mind

Gave my

soul to God ...

"I think I'm ...,

... a person now.

A service now (to something)

other than my hate.

Covered up my face

for the last time ...

"Gonna slash my
other cheek today."

ACT II

PORTALS

Trash Can Man

Below is the let go,

the "set go."

The never ending

said "no."

The best blow,

the quest home.

Triple feature

sex shows.

X rated...

In graves with

faces

enslaved with

stories of untold pain.

We of the summer time.

(How we $hine)

We of the true divine.

(World is mine)

Of mice and men

born again...,

here we're all

stone markings.

(Laced with cuts)

eyes wide shut...

fighting for

free parking.

This is the way

the world works...

This is the path

to circle jerks.

This is the plan

for constant hurt.

(This is today for us)

How do we counter

the countered?

12 steps ahead

they are.

Pray hard...,

we need an extra hand.

We can't scream

any louder!

Lost bets in hand

we are

claiming we're gods of man.

Ghosts of forbidden gods...

forbidding all,

to host

the lunar ball.

Galactic calls

out to all that cum.

Sedated and numb

we are

downgraded to bums.

"To a whole new world
I'll take you."

"It's safe to
(assume)

that this one's fucked."

They shot Christ...

Blew the top of His head off.

His skull formed a heart as it left His head.

His ears hung like horns.

This world will kill anything...,

even what's here to save it.

Dear children,

watch for falling

buildings.

(That's the world coming down)

This,

you see now

is fake.

It's all shapes

of paper

glued together.

Machines

control the weather.

No better,

we're off now

than whenever

this whole thing started.

(But I still believe in angels)

Disdainful...

men control

the time clock.

Tick, tock...

(a second closer to death)

Inept,

we are

with nothing left.

On to stars?

"Why?"

All we touch

dies...

"I hope we're not a cancer."

Into the sunset,

we go.

Into the show

(Our debut)

High side of low.

Let's break through

the unknown

and summon

a cyclone.

Graves of the unsaved...

relay...

calls for tidal waves

(to wash us out)

A holy cleansing...

A holy ending...

We are in the

age of empty.

Crosses on the ground,

(once carried)

Throwing in the towel,

unaware we

died many ages ago.

God of the slow

moving train of

insane brains

all begging for

decision.

Envision...,

a world of pure

understanding.

Rebranding...

ourselves

as forest elves

trying to get

our wings back.

Our wings black...

Here..., we're

the demons.

So many scars...

I guess I just wanted to show on the outside how I was feeling on the inside.

Placed where you are...

So lonely I used to call answering machines just to hear a voice in which to cry to.

Never the loved of much...

Never the safe to touch...

"I think I need a gas mask"

I can't grasp

a single breath in this place.

Not a single

head in this place

sees me as a person.

I need rest

from this place...

Need to get

the hell

out of this place.

Childhood...,

wrecked in this place.

(Fucking monsters.)

I don't understand

the closeness of a mother

or father.

I don't understand the bond.

What's it like

to belong?

Am I wrong...

to have nails

in my palms?

(Trying to connect to Jesus)

A cage in a cave...,

we're in.

We've been,

the most violent of all

with skin.

How do we change?

How do we hang

in...,

with a world this strange?

(Craving a fleet of hearses)

Trash Can Man

Reverse this

current coarse, please.

(We hate for purpose.)

Who's up there

pulling these strings?

On each dead world

I've marked a 6...,

left pictures of my dick

cumming.

Jerking with

slit wrists.

"Fuck this planet!"

Gnawing on

pussy lips.

(Nothing like a snuff film)

Hogging the inner hips

of every dead whore

lying in their own shit.

(It's what I'm here for)

Craving a menstruating

virgin...

and a full moon.

Craving a lot, lately...,

someone

I can run to.

Exit the 6 billion...

All of us,

lost children

Yes, I'm the reptilian

prince of broken peace.

Who's gonna fix

the leaks

when the storm comes?

Who's gonna change

the sheets?

So what's the point

of trying...

with timing

off and not

dividing...

up these creatures

evenly?

See in me,

nothing...

I'm trusting,

you'll hate me for

something.

This is the sad song

played

for the bad moms

saved

for the last bombs

we will ever see.

(Broke in a bottle)

I remember,

forgetting...

that which would topple.

(Now on the move)

Loose screws...

in every brain

of everything.

"Where do we find the creator?"

(His invention's gone wild)

An illegitimate child,

of the earth... I am.

(We are)

naked and vile,

on the last mile...

Here on the Sunday low.

Apocalypse

at hand...

(Death of a nail)

Street signs...

(Welcome to Hell)

The suicide hotline

hung up on me...

"Fucking jerks."

I know I'm not worth

shit..., but still, it hurts.

27 skies I see

in static.

27 rooms I'm in,

all padded.

"How did we ever advance?"

Tossing pennies...,

swollen,

stolen,

high rollin'

(I'm holding)

Tank is empty...,

pour me,

snort me,

get horny.

(I'm folding)

Don't resent me...,

bleeding,

breeding,

daydreaming.

(I'm trolling)

Pass the whisky...,

tripping,

fisting,

shape shifting.

(I'm golden)

Daring mine fields to trip me...

rip me...

to shreds

while getting head.

(I have the words for most)

A ghost...,

diagnosed

a fucking rock star

with my cock out.

Banging whores

in their south mouth.

(I am the words of most)

Suppose...

to smoke it up

and coast...

A toast,

to all of you

still hopeful.

"I wish you well."

A boat full

of people that hate

to sail.

Love in the middle...

"Fuck Chicken Little."

(There was never a sky to begin with)

Infection...

(unpleasant)

Conception...

(regretted)

Who would you trade me in for?

The clouds in the back are mountains.

The clouds in the front are not.

"They're ghosts."

(Electric)

Here, I'm the host...

(Elected)

to rule the psychotic.

(Enter the aquatic)

In vomit...

we'll make love.

Demonic...

are fake hugs.

Trust me...,

you shouldn't trust me.

(Everything about me's ugly)

Grieving the loss of sanity...

Pandering,

to those that want the Anti-

Christ

to be me.

"To be free?"

(Non existence)

To be 3...,

... again?

(won't risk it)

"Might get molested."

All dead end... roads

form one...

(future)

All dressed up... clones

are drug

(users)

We are the end

in color.

We are the rain

and thunder.

Give me a standing O!

I'm stoned

and here for you to spit on.

Seasonal depression...

(all 4 seasons)

How do we save the damaged when they're already
disadvantaged?

(69 steps in a circle)

... Dig the grave ...

(55 bets on the world)

... Won't be saved ...

"Foreseeable regression."

In the grand scheme of things...,

I'm still a piece of shit.

Pot of gold...,

melted.

In a hole...,

pelted

with garbage and

crucifixes.

My to do list

involves sanity...

and how not to lose it.

Those weren't clouds we saw in the sky, they were scrapes.

(I saw the blood)

I saw the paint... dripping.

(The night came late)

Honorary psychos,

here's your medal.

The devil

has plans for all.

Walking tall,

pissed and on call,

we bring the end of days.

Congratulate the dawn...,

(it made it through the night)

Roses...,

splinters...

disposing

December...

(Shaking the severed hand)

Praying that Neverland...,

(actually exists)

I need a kiss...

but got a fist...

(This is the planet now)

What happened to compassion?

(I guess it's out of fashion)

I need matches...

to light the uncompassionate

on fire...

(Just a reaction)

Oh well...

we're all scum anyways.

(Just bums hiding things)

"Who gives a fuck about us?"

A first round bust...,

we are...

but in the last round.

On 4th down

with a mile to go.

(No smile to show)

In style if bones

are what's in style...,

(starving for attention)

Closed yet open...

what's spoken's

been quoted

millions of years ago.

We're robots

thinking we're human.

Super advanced

yet stupid.

Not given

the full use of

the brain

for a reason.

We're demons...,

and this is hell.

We're semen...,

in wishing wells.

(Wishing to be ourselves)

but won't.

Abandon all hope.

The key broke

in the lock

and I can't pick it.

Here in stitches...,

my heart...

All needs fixing.

These scars...

grow in number each year.

Ever wanted to disappear?

(I'll help you)

The shell you

hide in

can be your home.

(Close the curtains...,

and never let anyone

know you're hurting)

"Me?"

"I'm not trying to hide."

"They'll feel my pain

till the universe dies."

(Just one of those things)

Fuck all...

and fuck laws

in place for their gain.

Gangbanged,

hookers

are true Americans.

True barbarians...

(the gods)

cosmic terrorist.

What can be simple here...,

when crippled here?

Our voices don't make sense.

We scream...,

but to a sound proof fence.

Who hears us?

Who's near us?

It seems we're all alone.

This cave is home

and we're just

an image shown.

An image loaned...,

from memories,

not our own...

"Welcome to dreamland."

Rumors afloat

of ghosts

getting too close

to teardrops.

Yes, God...,

we've destroyed ourselves again.

"It's what we have a knack for."

We're packed for

a one way journey

north.

Go ahead and set course...

"Here come the fallin angels."

Dear Victims...,

"Thank you for your service."

Blades along the trip wire...

This morning,

we're hunting...,

anything, something

that bleeds and feels

mistreated...,

that bleeds and needs

a beating...,

that grieves between the legs.

All are captives now...

... A sea beneath the bed...,

of God... that's filled with monsters.

If I gave up

would it matter

if it never mattered

anyway?

Have I mattered? (No)

I'm just a scarecrow

tied to a cross.

How do I get this off pause?

I've been here too long

and this song's

my favorite,

though it's dated.

(I'm wasted)

yet sober.

Feeling lower

than I ever have before.

Rotten

to the core.

Dropping

to the floor.

I can't do this anymore.

"You made me

an enemy...,

entering...,

prayers you have

for the end of me.

"God can't hear you now."

(Message intercepted)

"I'm to steer you now."

(Say goodbye to Heaven)

Say hello to zero.

Here with you in parts...

that were never me

but forever bleed.

These hands,

they hold you barely

with burdens

they cannot carry.

I am the final piece

of all

that disrupts sleep.

Here on the starting blocks...,

we take off

and face off

with our own reflection

while paid off

to lose.

Loose screws...,

in every human mind.

Use to's...,

in every walk of life.

"I feel like things are really about to

change... for the worse."

Get the hearse...,

in fact, get them all.

"A cleansing

will soon begin."

"Our ending

is groomed within."

We are a dying race...

We are a crying face...

The finish...

(we are)

A blemish...,

on the sands of time.

Trash Can Man

ACT III

GAMER

Trash Can Man

At church and

the preacher's

preaching

against me...

Telling the people

I'm evil,

empty...,

promises from a snake

For Heaven's sake,

don't curse me...

I'm thirsty

and reaching out.

I'm hurting

and seeking out

parts in this reality.

Scars...,

cry for a fatality.

I'm afraid

I'll never be me again.

(Whoever that is)

(Whoever this is)

More additions

to the mischief.

Heartless behavior we exhibit.

Are we even human beings still?

I don't have it in me to do this anymore.

Put down this book.

This battle...,

no look,

passes

passed away.

All in grey (colors)

Offensive to all.

"We have turned this world into a cesspool of disease and filth."

All of you I want to kill.

My heart hates equally.

Peacefully protesting

all I secretly

support.

No more favors dear children...

I'm out.

"Scout's honor."

Recount ... all your troublesome times

and see ... the one

pulling the strings

was me.

We're told we can be anything we want in a society that's already labeled us.

We're told who we are, what we are and what we'll be all before the age of 3.

Through cartoon propaganda, sitcom stereotypes and media manipulation.

By the age of 6 our minds are already encoded with failure or at best mediocrity.

Schools want us to achieve but only in their sports programs.

We're just numbers in a system of battery operated barcodes.

We're seen as nothing, told we're nothing, taught we're nothing..., so obviously we feel we're nothing.

We're told on a continuous basis that we don't matter..., that we're all worthless and that there's nothing we can do about it.

And strangely enough, the very lies that we have been brainwashed to believe is where we seem to be focusing our intellect therefore wasting it.

We look to a sky that's not there and wonder what's on the other side of it. We dream of exploring a frontier that doesn't even exist.

This world has become a cradle and we've become the helpless.

All by design, we've become..., undesigned.

We're on a level far above us and far below us all at the same time.

We're more intelligent than we're led to believe but unaware of it due to the locks put on our minds.

The day we break free will never come cause the masses will never accept the truth outside the dream.

Only the individual can do this and once done will be labeled as crazy by the same masses of fools whose lives exist in paper entertainment, plastic satisfaction and electric Armageddon.

Who's dressed up

for the show?

(The first act)

"Christ comes back

and has a heart attack"

...Salvation delayed...

Exit the stage...,

left...

Gone are the blessed

(No place for them)

If earth had a neck...,

I'd break it.

We are the second zero...

The fallen.

The bloodline of Nero...

dissolved and

put on display

for tourists.

Call me Caligula...,

the saint.

St. Caligula.

My reign...

the greatest

since Zeus.

No use,

for those that

hand out abuse.

(Modern day peasants)

My Christmas present...

to the world

is me...,

dying on Christmas.

Will I miss this? "No."

The world

hates me

like an aborted

baby

with its spine snapped.

In mice traps,

we are.

Just no bars...

cause it's mental

and we're simple

minded

missiles

guided

by TV control.

"Most would trade souls

to the devil."

"My blood vessels

seem to be moving

poison."

Buried beneath stars...

(In loss columns)

Scared we may break apart.

This new Sodom.

The grand bottom.

Barely a beating heart.

All images projected...,

all paths chosen.

In this dome

that'll never open.

We're lines in stone,

stoned..., doing lines.

Grabbing vines,

hoping for a strong one.

Hoping there's no bottom

called Hell.

Hard to say what I feel or felt.

"I'm just static in this era of melodramatic tells."

"And no climatics or things considered tragic

are of use anymore."

"We've become dolls."

(Pushers of invisible wars)

"Is there really

an enemy

or just

an audience

to die for?"

"Who's on the balcony tonight?"

"Who's in the press box?"

"The nosebleeds are packed."

"Who has a guest spot?"

What if the truth is something that was forgotten a very long time ago and by seeking it..., we're really just digging more into the lie?

Deception from all directions

"These are the times we've dreaded."

(Expecting the unexpected)

"Taught that we're just infections."

...They listen to us cry...

I exist without existing. You need me but don't know it. There's a shield around the moon that won't open. Stays closed and..., knows of the outside beasts

that'll never be released from the chains until trained in the art of environment. The know of the Gods..., the growth. The oath in a pause. There's still a sun outside. Grow. No truth in school halls.

Here with bags,

packed.

Ready to disappear.

"It's time to transcend."

My skin...,

everyone

it seems to offend.

We are the eye of the storm.

The center...

The taken form...

The inner

self

of new creation,

encased with

the latest

upgrades and changes.

"When do we get to heaven...,

or are we already here

and just making it hell?"

When the magic wears off...,

you'll know it.

"Enjoy the mischief."

Enriched with

nothing but

bad intentions.

"People are the same everywhere."

(Leaches)

"People are insane everywhere."

Speeches...,

of hate now a popular thing.

Let's just kill everyone

"Fuck it."

Let's just fill everyone

up with

bullets then eat

their faces.

The famous...,

first to go in cages

going off a cliff.

It's not a hit list,

it's a wish list

for Santa

on Christmas.

No toys...,

just throats slit.

Goodbye to

many millions...,

billions...

Fuck it!

Reptilian

monsters

most now are.

Ghosts of Mars

haunt me...

Shots ring...,

out when vision

visits.

Enter in this...,

maze of hits

and misses.

How many bells in hell?

"We of the flattened circle."

How many fortunes tell

truth that's

universal?

Hidden by human hands,

a conqueror,

history calls

a philosopher.

Home of the blood offer...

(here)

Dreams of my real father,

(clear)

"It's time to be a serpent."

Trash Can Man

Straight lines have laws

"Escape them."

Stay high or fall

(It's protocol)

Grey skies have walls

"Deface them."

We're paper balls

in burning dolls.

Nowhere we feel

we're safe at.

Have we evolved

any at all?

No home to be

in place at.

No rooms, no halls,

no lights, no calls

All over nowhere

in rhythm.

Symbolism...,

cuts through the

rotting brain.

A losing game,

we're in

if choosing fame

(to worship)

Allergic...,

to truth.

So many are...,

useful idiots.

Waking in separate

mornings.

Naked and craving

glory.

Led by a cumshot...

(wrapped, packaged)

and sold as a new thought.

This is the end

of now...

in sequence.

"This is the falling down."

Somewhere in sadness...

there's captives

with smiles

reacting

to vile

hand drawn situations.

On trial...,

humanity.

Worthwhile...,

insanity.

We are

the holy way

for slaves

in demonic

parades.

Master of ceremony...,

come to.

Laughter in purgatory...,

(lungs blue)

Sever the cords

around you, please do.

"It's our turn to be god."

There's no movement

on this ball...,

it's flat.

In back,

the outside

is black

with peach skies

calling itself

the night.

"I wonder if Eve ate here?"

The grapes here

are toxic.

Erased here

are options.

We have the hands of killers...,

saving...

that which never changes.

"Look at the clouds,

their mouths...,

waiting to take us in."

(So be it)

Hating we're in this skin.

(Must leave it)

"Fearing we're at the end."

No one's out there in spaceships

to save us..., steal us...,

rape us or kill us.

Just stations...,

providing facelifts

fill the void.

Hacked droids,

fill the pulpits.

The culprits...,

all look like me.

Just might be,

the culprit.

Unfold it...,

the map.

(It shows where the soul's at)

No facts...,

in this world.

Just cracks.

"The man in the mirror

is sick."

Back to back nightmares on back to back nights for many...

(Never a wet dream)

Preachers say,

we're going to hell

for everything.

In every brain,

a smile that hides

in pain.

My name...,

hates it's attached

to me.

Hates to react

to me.

Feels there's no match

with me.

Sleeps in the cracks

of me.

"Guess I'm going nowhere."

We're right at home

when lost

and comfortable in ruin.

Pursuing twisted thoughts.

Confused beneath

this fluid

(we call the sky)

Want three sixes?

Take them.

Mayhem...

comes from

misread kisses.

Brain stem's

filled with hits

and misses.

Pain filled...,

words address

the senses.

"How bout another...,

shit covered

town to start a cult in?"

I'll be your god...,

I promise...,

as long as you're

my goddess.

"How bout another...,

shit covered

whore to put a dream in?"

I'll take your pain...,

and bleed it

then mix it with

my semen.

"Call me the cure."

For sure,

no victors here...

just fear.

(We sabotage ourselves)

Who still has a conscience?

Is there anything stronger than a text book lie?

A lie so big that it's basically common sense to support it.

A lie so big that if it was even just slightly questioned, the one doing the questioning would be seen as a lunatic.

Well..., unfortunately there are. (Millions of them)

We call these lies history.

We call these lies facts.

We even kill to protect these lies and wash our hands of anyone who dares open their eyes.

We're so afraid of the truth that we would rather live in the lie because it's more comfortable for us.

We're so afraid of thinking for ourselves that we let others do it for us.

These are how the lies get started and why they go unchallenged.

It's like we're in some kind of demonic wet dream getting ass raped..., begging for more.

Forget that we're torn open.

Forget that we need stitches.

Forget it's a snuff film ending

with three sixes.

We keep asking for it.

We keep admiring those

who are giving it to us.

We'd rather be trendy than be ourselves.

We'd rather be empty than see what else

could be there to fill us up.

How did we get so sad and why?

When?

Can any of you see the fight

we're in?

Battle after battle,

victim after victim.

Here we sleep beaten...,

born casualties of the system.

Focused on nothing

but my next cum shot.

The best I've got,

gotten..., many years ago.

Many moons have shown

up for this occasion.

This relation-

ship shipped out

rotation.

"Call me the painted night."

A pain that I

live with...,

the pain of time.

We of the golden lock...

tarnished.

We of the spurting cock.

"The garden of Eden still exists."

"We call it Earth."

Walk on this razor with me.

The blade is smooth

with room for two.

The news

just got here

today.

They say

the earth said

fuck this place.

Lay on this razor with me.

The edge is us

before it cuts.

The trust

issues are

the same.

No brain

can say it's

not insane.

Followed by the feeling of

a cold chill.

This whole field...,

(covered with land mines)

We're all sealed...

(up with the end times)

"Who still feels?"

Can tyrants be blamed for being tyrants if that's what they were raised to be?

What else do they know aside from what they were taught?

Evil or necessary evil?

"Maybe people need to be ruled."

"Look at how we treat ourselves."

No direction wants us

unless to hunt us.

"We are a hated bunch."

It is what it is

when it was

as it should be.

The would be

coming of

open eyes

could see

a world that's

paralyzed.

"We're not ready for truth."

"It's too...,

heavy for us

to move."

(Bring back the clowns)

A shift is needed.

(Just the first round

and already bleeding)

"What've we gotten into?"

Akin to...,

dirt.

Here in this

curse.

"Did we ever stand a chance?"

Trash Can Man

ACT IV

ATONEMENT

Trash Can Man

The rivers

remember

the shivers

of sinners.

Forgivers

deliver

a bitter

avenger.

My message

is wreckage.

Oppressive

progressives.

Aggressive

depressants

are dressing

our essence.

The innocence from children is all we have left to show
we're human. Without it, we're just monsters that should be
killed off.

The face of God is in a baby's smile.

Fuck Hollywood.

Programs of progress

fill us.

Showdowns with promise

kill us.

We are the liar's liar.

We are the sick and tired.

(Diving into can't waits)

(Fucking on the first date)

Doing things best in fire.

"Call up the warm and fuzzy...,

shit's about to get ugly."

Here for the keeping...

Breathing...

only cause we're told to.

The cold moves

freely..., empty.

(As it is controlled to)

The roll through

bleeds these..., feelings.

(Hard to get a hold to)

The toll booth's

reaching..., kneeling.

(Begging for a gold tooth)

"I am the one

you've been waiting on."

(Head of the new dawn)

(A love song...,

written to steal your heart)

Making my mark...

bringing you back from dark.

"Giving you all the lead."

On scabbed knees,

you'll all be, blowing me.

(Triple X fanatics)

... make magic ...

(Triple X climactics)

Wanna kill and save

humanity...

(I love and hate)

"Extinction...,

on its way."

The final face...,

will see

the resting place

of we...,

the people.

All over

this realm...,

a graveyard.

We failed

to save our-

selves again.

"Needing a prequel and a reboot."

A redo...,

for thieves who

wish their dreams

weren't see through.

"You bleed, too?"

(Hadn't noticed)

At home but still feel

homeless.

"Where did my mother go?"

It's hopeless...,

trying to find another.

No brothers

or sisters

or cousins,

just figures...

in black shared voices

with me.

"How do I let it go?"

"How can I face the snow?"

(The cold's always bothered me)

"At 4, this world altered me."

(A miracle I've not murdered...,

or have I?)

The bad guy's

on stand by,

saving for a nuke.

"We're in the final chapter."

"We are the never after."

Stitches can't hold

ashes to gold.

"We are the end in sequence."

"We are the way to grievance."

Stitches can't take

tears off the face.

"We'll all be one when we're dead."

(Call it the black rainbow)

A past gameshow

stuck on repeat.

"No winners this week."

(The fix was in)

Dents within...

sleep,

creep

up.

Keep

us...

out of the dark right now

cause we're

begging for hearts right now.

Meaning (not meaning as much)

There's no such...

thing

as

another us.

The other us...

feels the same way, too.

Sealed their own fate, too.

(We're all fucked)

Screams of "I hate you"

coming from the mirror.

"What if we're the reflection and what we see as the
reflection is reality...,

judging us?"

Open up...,

it's time to take your meds.

Sober up...,

the climb may break your legs.

This level...,

not meant for most.

A toast...,

to my future ghost.

(Don't look back in anger)

I guess we're still here...,

wherever "here" is.

Never clear is...

the picture.

Less fears

of

the scripture.

"Priests preach bleach to the sleep-

ing... weeping..., beaten souls in need...,

of color.

(Notice the rainbow)

It's covered...,

with beauty.

Smothered...

with soothing

calm... right after storm.

(What does it really mean?)

In scenes...,

trying to flip the script.

Claiming we're human.

(Faking our movement)

Usage...,

manipulated.

Truth is...,

we're in cages.

Painted

and filled with props.

Sealed with locks...,

(all doors)

Filled with shots.

"Stay the fuck in."

"The outside hates you."

Eyes betray you...

(Room of collapsing squares)

I must tear...

out this demon heart.

Possession...

Six took over

seven.

Regression...,

of the mind

(a weapon)

Depression,

battles...

I wish to exit.

A veteran,

I am at these affairs.

Back to the nightmare...

we'll go

once the software

downloads.

Call it a day in the life of...

what dies of

starvation.

"The world's on fire."

(Cremation)

Headlines says "Dire

Situations

All Over!"

My shoulder...,

sore from punching mirrors.

"Is the coast clear?"

(Never was)

Dirt is on my windshield.

Every walk of life

has steps

on a killing field.

Every breath of day

opens graves

for the concealed

weapons of the dark.

(Weaponizing hearts)

Driving through the rain, stoned..., feels like flying...,

rising

at least a step.

Climbing

up out this mess.

(Hoping to find an outside)

The inside...

does not like

the sunshine.

(Headlights show a tunnel)

Night time walls

crumble.

(Rain above me speaks)

Seeks..., retribution

for the leaks.

Each tear...,

a painting

making waves.

"The unchained...,

rip apart the ocean."

"The renamed...,

play out in the open."

(Calling a special conference

on how to keep a promise)

I'm thinking of laying low

till it's show-

time. Rewind.

I'm thinking of slaying foes

till there's no

more. Restored...,

peace the best of all.

The less of all...

within me...,

and blessing all.

Order out of chaos

We're not living,

we're drifting.

Resisting

what's fitting

for us as

a species.

(In feces

for freebies)

Disease cause

we're diseased

creatures in

deep sleep.

The best of us

go early.

The rest of us

don't worry

about anything

outside the nursery.

(On beaten paths)

Inside we're hurting.

"This season pass

goes year 'round."

All down

with the ref close to ten.

Needing a second wind

(to kick in)

"Grieving for all with skin."

Battle lines drawn.

Battle plans laid out.

Gave out ... my heart,

(it did)

Played out...

(this world)

Flames crowd the center.

Will we remember ...

anything?

(Supernatural)

Nothing's factual.

Here we all stand in lines waiting ...

for an actual ... life.

Turn the machine off...

"It's noisy."

Here's an obscene shot of my cock...

straight pointing north.

(Never on course) Are we...

ever remorseful?

The landslide's coming ...

(We asked it)

Hearts patented away.

(Heads blasted)

"Who wants to be a junkie?"

Filling tummies... with semen.

Steady cumming.

They're not laughing with you.

They're laughing at you.

A crap shoot (everyday)

Every second ... wondering ...

"Will I make it to Heaven?"

"Everything coming ...

we've brought on ourselves

and deserve everything coming

to us."

Monsters...,

at every red light.

(No turns)

Every said fight ... coming ...,

we've earned.

(Every head sniped)

This is the was and will be.

Rebuilding ... nothing.

Just filthy ... (and owning it)

Guilty ... and knowing it.

The innocent?

"Fuck 'em!"

"They're belligerent."

So how many licks

on the tootsie pop?

Guess I'm not wanted

for the guest spot.

The test caught ... me off guard.

"All bets off."

(I think we're just chasing air)

Going bare ... back.

I think we're just taking care...,

of everything.

(Showing wear) Cracks ...

all over these leather seats.

I never sleep ... it seems.

(I can't)

Too many bad dreams.

Decapitated and still taking facials.

Still turning tables

(on all things)

Still letting cables sleep.

To be ... (or not to)

... Always the question.

(No heading)

"Always rejected."

Replacing sevens with sixes.

Blessing the twisted minds.

(Here lie the gifted)

Kissed and uplifted ...

No longer the fisted.

Ass sore no more

rich kids...,

finally...

"Poisoning lunch kits."

Far beyond driven ...

Incisions ..., (self-made)

Self-sprayed ... we are ...,

self-laid... to rest.

(Invade the deep)

I see ...

all sorts of things while cumming.

"Off coarse..., it seems

we're always running."

(Perfectly drowning)

Perfectly counting down the days for all.

"Purposely doubted."

Not good for anyone

... or anything.

Just here so flapping tongues

can gain wings...,

sound brave,

... (spew hate)

I can't relate (to any of you)

"Don't want to."

Can't even say we're trying anymore.

Shutting doors...

Cutting cords.

But can't afford to unravel.

This battle ... expensive.

Like cattle ... we're fenced in.

(Trusting the butchers)

Laying bare. Unaware ...

... that we're hookers,

plugged into outlets.

Drugged and needin' counselin'

Who says you can't go home?

(Here in bones ... aching)

Games for thrones ... shaking ...

up this whole damn world.

I was going to come

but left ...

(never meaning to stay)

Trash Can Man

I was thinking I'm young

then wept.

(Rolling to fade)

Showing a weaker second...

The speaker's question

really made me think.

(Fade now blink)

"What reality is this?"

"Who's?"

Up on the balcony

a shooter.

Earth movers ...,

killed by social media.

They won't grieve for ya' ...

even if you bleed for 'em.

This need for torturing

(erotic)

Here's a scream for ya'.

Just toxic behavior everywhere.

(Robotic)

All hands on deck ...

We must get

(out of here)

Cigar-ette lit.

(Last one)

Narrative changing.

Trash Can Man

We're all in ropes

... hanging.

Famous the internet made us all.

(Hurricane Shadow)

Teddy bear psychos ...

Type o's

(on purpose)

Sideshows

all current.

We are a breath of air

floating...,

hoping

we're going

in something that cares.

Here for the comments only.

Here for the hatred.

Takes me away from my own problems.

Maybe...

I'm perfect.

Encouraged by all others

lack of nourishment.

(Throwing curves to centers.)

Hitler ..., alive in most.

"Have we've ever been more hateful?"

Too many Kane's ...

Too few Able's.

All attractions ... fatal.

Watch your step

around me ...

The counseling's (not working)

Caught flirting (with a handgun)

A new drug (habit)

A flu bug

for all.

"Come catch me."

Undressing

the world with my eyes.

Rejecting ...,

most of what it says.

A certified user ...

a verified loser.

Terrified.

Left behind.

Vilified

accusers ... accusing

undoings

on God.

(All fueding)

Mass shootings

everywhere.

"No gluing this thing

together."

Never say

"God didn't send a messenger."

(I'm here)

Heart beats irregular

when near (anyone)

Rule of thumb?

"Fuck it."

Cruel are crumbs (when hungry)

Every second now ... seems quicker,

seems bitter ...,

seems a twin to all quitters

(needing skin)

Remembered...,

for all the wrong reasons.

Only calm when sleeping ...

until I start dreaming

and start seeing

every human face screaming,

bleeding ... unaware that it's me

that's the demon ...

(they're tortured by)

Confetti falling.

Street walking ...

stalking ... everyone.

"Call me a vigilante."

Hidden hands we ...,

need to uproot.

Need to reboot

(we're offset)

Need to reshoot

this scene.

We're in too deep.

See? Tricks aren't just

for kids.

Sucks we didn't

remember what we saw coming.

Just things running (we are)

Hoping it's to something.

Solutions..., temporary.

(Here waiting)

Flicking lights, in fear saying ...

"Bloody Mary!"

Something scary ... this way comes

(and wicked)

Somethings buried ...

Unrepentant ..., most

Just defendants ...,

we all are.

(Bad for business)

Who will the assassins be?

Caption seeks ... words

screaming action.

Keeping stacks of insults

near ...

Leaving tracks.

"Time to get out of here."

Sleeping bag

has a snake in it.

Not a place in the

world for me.

Escape..., made for it.

(No escaping)

Faces facing

off with

mirrors breaking.

Seems we're taking

our sweet time with everything

devastating.

Not really knowing who any of you are anymore...,

(and not caring)

These thoughts very...

carefully ... caress me

when I'm terribly

messed up

from daring

to be myself.

Maybe that's why ... my eyes stay closed to you ...

They're supposed to.

Judgement rushing,

crushing ...

blood sucking.

Soon coming (to us)

dungeons.

Who just ...,

turned the lights off?

I might off

many.

This?

(My fight song)

Patch me through to emergency.

Seems we're all in a hurry

to die.

Future's not blurry

to me.

It's 20/20.

Roads are bumpy

and only getting worse.

Only seeing dirt ... now.

Someone call the nurse.

(We may need a doctor)

Screams to the Father ...

"Please help us!"

(Dreams of the somber)

We're all underwater ..., hoping someone

bothered ...,

to turn the filter on.

Decomposing shells...,

(falsely painted)

Plaintiffs...,

everywhere.

Maintenance (needed)

Come tomorrow

will we still be breathing?

Seems like everyone's on the run

(though innocent)

Seems like everything's one and done.

So on to the next drug habit.

The next mass stabbing.

The next Alice in Wonderland chasing the white rabbit.

So many dropped caskets ...

(too many to count)

Guest unannounced, we all are ...,

hexed, soon to bounce.

I saw children standing next to a fire. They were reaching up to me. I could see their bodies but not their faces.

Whenever I tried to look at their faces, their mouths would stretch across their heads.

It ended with me seeing fields of them. All next to a fire, reaching up to me. All of their faces turned to mouths screaming.

I don't know how to help them.

In reverse ... hitting

where it hurts.

(Fast forward)

Past horrors

bare the urn.

Scared of turns (backwards)

Paired with burns.

Guilty...,

in all ways

meaning filthy.

Building ...,

nothing but silly feelings

for all that's really (not here)

No mirror sees me.

No tear cures bleeding.

Stop signs on mute.

(Not stopping)

All flopping.

(Call a tech)

Here shopping

for the end of all.

Stocking up on

things to fall from.

Think we're all zom-

bies now ...,

(hoodwinked)

Farewell to all.

Off pause ... this game is.

(Lost cause) ... My name is

back on the hit list

of this cocked gun.

Don't care if

I'm hated.

(I am anyway)

Saving ...

plenty face.

Breaking ...

many chains.

Praying (for)

many things.

(All beneficial)

Nothing's simple.

Hypnotic visuals

taking over.

Making over

everything.

Throw me

back in the womb.

"I'm homesick."

My bones just

don't move

(like they use to)

A moment in time.

One moment I'm fine ...,

then not.

I just got

through one mood swing

now I'm back in another.

Dad's rubber ..., broke

the night he got my mother

(pregnant)

At least that's how he acted.

Here and back in

this rut again.

These cuts they give me

reason ...

A belief in something

other than demons.

Disbanded ...

(Our way of life)

Low chance in

getting it back together.

No sweater

and it's cold outside.

Chain letters ...

take a toll on time.

Who's trending now?

(Air bending?)

Care's shifting into

hairs splitting.

Spitting ...,

at everyone.

Grinning with every gun

pointed at the world.

No honest men left...,

just rocket men.

I wish I could be the hero.

The years, though

(doing me in)

Appears ghosts (are)

stronger than men.

"I may be afraid of everything."

"This may be a cage."

What stage (of this level) are we on?

What page of the book?

Follow me.

Come swallow me.

I'm on the way up now

and I've got my make up (on)

World ...,

needs a shake up.

(A war)

Parts 3 and 4

coming.

Asleep no more.

There's a reason for

everything, I guess.

Who you preaching for?

Screaming for

many ones.

(Heartbeats to rain drops)

I'm famous

nowhere.

Just contagious.

Fuck the faces

that use me!

A new me

here now

for booing.

So boo me!

Amused by

undoings.

Defusing

no bombs.

Reusing

these palms

for more nails to be driven through.

Missing screws inside me.

Getting use to hiding.

Letting loose.

"Come find me."

Wetting news teams up.

I'm trying ...

not to be a killer.

But the pillars holding my walls are cracking

and lacking compassion..., I am.

Don't give a damn anymore.

Fixed scores ...

controlled this game from the start.

We die for pennies.

Broke with empty

(stomachs)

Cloaked with sins we wish we didn't have.

(Wish we didn't know)

"Now we just tiptoe ...

around everything."

(Now we just slit throats)

A shit show

on a train ... crashing ...

with us grabbing ...

razors instead of rails.

(Our minds cracking)

Eyes dragging (on)

smiles sagging.

Not asking for much here.

Just passing

the time.

(No faces)

Basing ...,

saviors on "heads or tails."

Pages in books mark conversation.

Each, a moment in time ... continued.

Each, a person in line ... waiting.

I think I'll try

a little harder today.

Both ways I'll look (so)

don't say I took

anything for granted.

Just candid (cameras)

around us.

No stamps of approval.

We're all cuts

on the wrist of God

when hating.

Demonstrating ...,

only ...

what we see

is phony.

"I long for a smile."

(A real one)

These pills bum

me out.

(I feel numb)

Better reel some

fish in soon,

(I'm starving)

Departing ...

(this world)

Bizarre things

ahead.

What ever happened to consideration?

It seems we're taking

more lives than making.

(Earth is quaking)

Seems we're all saying

"Fuck it."

Not praying

anymore (are we?)

Clark Kent ... missing.

Superman ...,

where are you?

It's all doom

and gloom now.

We're all through

(being kind)

There's no room

for neighbors.

(All strangers)

Ball breakers

everywhere.

Naysayers

in church.

Never in first place.

(Outcomes reversed)

"We need hatred to sell."

Hallucinating ...,

playing pin the tail

on the zombie.

Unabombing ...,

everything.

Hurricane...,

(coming)

War drums ... bumping.

"Hit 'em harder."

Shotgun's pumping.

Whole world's hunting.

Mapping fates.

(Using illusion)

A shoe in ... for destruction.

No peep shows here ...

just creep shows.

Asleep though most are.

(No cheat mode)

I wish I had love for everyone...

but don't ...

(Head's apart now)

I'm a dart now ... flying.

Hang gliding

to the outside.

Stalling ...

We're still men, right?

(No loose ends)

The noose bends slightly.

No more shiny ... happy people.

No more climbing ...,

... to nowhere.

The ropes tear when touched.

No host here.

The boats here

have holes in them.

A hoax steers us all.

Not caring I'm a freak.

Mystique ...,

morphing into me.

Pouring into me

vast realms.

Past selves ...

coming back to life.

My tusk stays ... low

I must stray away.

I just prayed

(for everyone)

to worship me.

The worst of me

running

from the hurt in me.

No courtesy coming,

just burning things.

World's wide open

(Anal gaped)

World's cries going ...,

nowhere.

World's eyes soaking

us up ... Good luck too all

and goodnight.

These times (changing like a motherfucker)

In the rain, trying to stay covered.

Who will I be tomorrow?

Who will I need?

Doors are shut to ...

all faces now.

(The night changes)

Denied placement ...

in this world.

Denied space ships ...

to leave.

I see (devils)

all around me.

New breeds (of terror)

To flee or not to ...

Soon to fall through

multiple ceilings.

Told that we're demons

(by monsters) ...

Holes that we'll be in ...

The future is a mixed one ...

yet fixed ...

Blips on this radar

throwing fits.

Knowing it's (about to explode)

Stoning kids ...

for views.

(Fluids move)

Rubik's cubes (together)

juicing boos.

Just make sure you're watching.

Ungodli (ness) rules.

Cleared for brainwashing.

Name calling ...,

we're back to.

Things falling ...

apart.

Not faulting the stars

for being there.

Just salty from scars.

Hoping that arms (won't push me)

into alarms.

Give my regards

to the scoundrels.

High councils (say)

the hounds will

sniff us out.

What's the line here?

"I'm lost."

Charged a fine here ...

for breathing.

16 seeds we (are) ...

... sixteenth.

All pink

on the inside.

All think

about things

we'd hang for.

We're stained for

other's sins.

Grandmother's kid (a witch)

No cover in

the playhouse.

Rise and shine.

It's doomsday.

Suit and tie (required)

You and I vs. fire.

A million to one (tenth)

Hunted ...,

like a cockroach,

busted ... in the light.

On the ropes ...

bobbing, weaving,

trading beatings ...

Bell ring yet?

Lots of bleeding's (occurred)

Billions screaming

for my death.

Here the villain

for all.

"You're welcome."

I'll take a bow now.

Rebellion ... coming.

We fail if nothing

comes from our lives.

Some can see time

unbitten.

Most can sell lies...

to children.

No more reasons for handshakes.

Can't stand fakes.

Can't stand snakes.

Undertaker coming

with tombstones.

I sued home

for negligence.

The youth is

my proof.

No scooting this way.

No moving.

All grooving

to violence.

All choosing

to kill.

Had my fill (of faces)

Just cold chills in public.

Can't tug it (my dick here)

No lovin' ... allowed.

We're down

and the clock's almost out.

Almost loud enough

but still no sound.

"I feel a draft here."

Get packed we're

moving away from past years.

No cracked mirrors

to see us.

No maps here.

Admittance?

Not getting!

"Good riddance."

No visits allowed.

No bigots.

Hear crickets.

Last minute (changes)

Stabbed infants...,

we all are.

"Welcome to the next scene."

Acts 1 through 3

Trapped (within)

all 4 of me.

Now forwarding

your call ...,

concern ...

"Dollhouse burned up last night

and I'm holding the matches."

Covering cuts

with scratches.

(Hovering madness)

Here in this palace

of exile.

Here in this tragic (comedy)

"We're all being played for fools here."

The new year (came) a year too late.

It's time to shake

the garden.

Need a pardon (from God)

Need restarting.

No roads open.

Not going (anywhere anyway)

Close to throwing in

the towel.

(Burned too many times)

Not a person in anyone's eyes.

(Just perversion)

Sermons against me.

Curses prevent me

from ridding serpents.

A burden to everyone it seems.

A circus

(sideshow)

All on trial.

Going viral for all things,

homicidal.

All with files (a mile long)

Death's in style.

Sky's out

(and not coming back on)

"Time out!"

Keep hearing sad songs...,

(repeating in my head)

Dreaming once again ...,

of hiding bodies.

Thinking naughty (thoughts)

because they're free.

No cuts in scenes (here)

"All fucked on screen."

"Tryin to find a top."

A clock (that will slow down)

We're not (here) I think.

Just dots here...,

pissing in bottles.

X'd out ...

Put a neck out (for too long)

Ain't got a head now.

"The world's crying shoulder."

All burning beds now.

Don't see a me that's older.

"Fuck it!"

I'm turning heads now.

The outside of in.

The bending of shifts.

(A truth to pretend)

The blending of six.

(Seeing triple)

The mixing of bits

(and pieces)

Not a care "So what?"

or a share (in the market)

Bout to start a fire here.

Bout to char the (world)

"Who wants a fresh prince?"

"Who wants their neck licked?"

(Still trying to make a difference)

Honorably mentioned ...,

dishonorably.

What if this is limbo...,

and these choices are our last?

No cast (on this world)

yet it's broken.

Through masks,

they steer us...

with tags

(on clearance)

"Time to end this masquerade."

This mask I made

reflects the

test we fail.

Lord, help me.

"Can't pass another test."

Will there be a next time to get to?

I miss you.

Hope to see you (next time)

Hope to kiss you

in the morning.

Unless you're mourning for me.

The warnings (everywhere)

Exploring an outcome.

Mouths run ...,

constantly.

(Growls come)

Bowels hung

up to dry.

Out 1.

"Two more to go."

A drink for the road.

(It's goodbye)

The bright side of evening...,

still sleeping.

"Tonight? ... ...

We become beautiful."

www.ingramcontent.com/pod-product-compliance
Lightning Source LLC
Chambersburg PA
CBHW032052080426
42733CB00006B/249